DATE DUE

NOV 2 3 2007	
MAY 0 4 2008	

VANISHING RAIN FOREST

RAIN FORESTS

Lynn Stone

The Rourke Corporation, Inc.
Vero Beach, Florida 32964

Printed in the U.S.A.

PHOTO CREDITS
All photos © Lynn M. Stone

Library of Congress Cataloging-in-Publication Data

Stone, Lynn M.
   The vanishing rain forest / by Lynn M. Stone
      p. cm. — (Discovering the rain forest)
   Includes index
   ISBN 0-86593-395-2
   1. Rain forest ecology—Juvenile literature. 2. Rain forests—
Juvenile literature. 3. Deforestation—Tropics—Juvenile literature.
[1. Rain forests. 2. Rain forest ecology. 3. Rain forest
conservation. 4. Ecology.]
   I. Title   II. series: Stone, Lynn M.   Discovering the rain forest.
QH541.5.R27S77 1994
574.5'2642—dc20   94-20910
                                                                      CIP
Printed in the USA   AC

TABLE OF CONTENTS

THE VANISHING TROPICAL RAIN FOREST

Tropical rain forests are warm, wet wonderlands of green plants and strange animals. Scientists believe that more than half of all the **species**, or kinds, of plants and animals on Earth live in tropical rain forests.

Many of the tropical rain forest plants and animals are still unknown to scientists. Unfortunately, some of these plants and animals may never be known. They are disappearing right along with the tropical rain forests themselves.

Destruction of tropical rain forest takes a heavy toll of plants and animals

SLIPPING AWAY...

The world's tropical rain forests cover a huge area, perhaps seven percent of the world's land surface. But large chunks of the forests are being cut, bulldozed and burned.

Many of the tropical countries that have rain forests need additional open land. Rain forests are destroyed to make room for farm crops, cattle, roads and homes.

No one knows exactly how much rain forest is being destroyed each year. One guess is that it's an area the size of West Virginia.

Cleared rain forest opens land for roads, farms and homes

WHERE THE RAIN FORESTS ARE

Tropical rain forests grow in the warmth and wetness of lands on or near the **equator**. The biggest tropical rain forest is in South America. One South American country, Brazil, has nearly one-third of the world's entire tropical rain forest!

West Africa, Southeast Asia and Central America also have large tropical rain forests. Scattered tropical rain forests are in southern Mexico, northeastern Australia and on islands in the Caribbean Sea and South Pacific Ocean.

Tropical rain forests grow in a wide band around the Earth's equator

USING THE RAIN FORESTS' RESOURCES

Most of the world's remaining rain forests are not protected. Each nation is free to use its tropical rain forests as it wants.

Many nations believe their rain forests are worth more "dead" than "alive." For example, a country can make money quickly by selling its rain forest trees for **lumber**.

Sometimes huge blocks of rain forest are destroyed by logging. All the trees are cut down. Logging can also be done carefully. Only the best trees are selected for cutting. The rest—much of the forest—are left.

Cutting and hauling rain forest trees provide jobs in tropical countries

The loss of rain forests threatens far more species than just the blue and gold macaw

Scientists work to discover and learn about rain forest plants and animals before they disappear

FOREST TO FARM

Most nations with tropical rain forests need more food and more open land for their growing populations. Ground that once grew forest is now producing cattle, coffee or another crop.

Former rain forest land rarely makes good farmland. Rain forest soil is not very **fertile**, or rich. After just a few years of farm use, the soil is almost useless for growing crops. That often means that more rain forest will be cut.

Cattle graze on a hillside once covered by tropical rain forest

THE USEFUL TROPICAL RAIN FORESTS

A healthy tropical rain forest is good for everyone. The plants in the forest help keep the air clean. They keep air temperatures steady. The plants keep soil in place so that it doesn't **erode** and dirty streams.

A healthy rain forest also supports an amazing number and variety of living things.

16

Healthy tropical rain forest prevents erosion and supports a huge variety of plants and animals

THE RAIN FOREST AND WEATHER

Tropical rain forest has an impact on Earth that reaches far beyond the forest's borders. Consider the high **humidity**, or moisture, of the tropical rain forest. That moisture escapes into the **atmosphere**, Earth's blanket of air. Moisture in the atmosphere is healthy.

When tropical rain forest is destroyed, the Earth's weather patterns may be changed.

A thin cloud of moisture hangs over the rain forest "roof"

THE GREENHOUSE EFFECT

Many scientists are afraid the Earth's atmosphere is becoming too warm. Like a greenhouse, the atmosphere may be trapping heat that would not ordinarily be there. Scientists call the warming of the atmosphere the Greenhouse Effect.

Burning of rain forests may be especially harmful. Burning, whether it is coal, oil, or trees, warms the atmosphere.

If the Earth's atmosphere is warming, it could some day begin to melt polar ice. That would mean higher oceans and flooded coasts.

Slashing and burning of rain forests may add to the warming of Earth's atmosphere

VANISHING PLANTS AND ANIMALS

When rain forest is even partly destroyed, some of the plants and animals disappear. The danger is that some of these species may not live in any other rain forest. As tropical rain forest vanishes, we lose some of the plants and animals we haven't even found yet!

Plants and animals that become **extinct**—disappear forever—can't be replaced. And some of them might have been of special value to people.

Glossary

atmosphere (AT muss feer) — the "blanket" of air around the Earth

equator (ee KWAY ter) — the line drawn on maps around the Earth's middle at equal distances from the north and south poles

erode (ee RODE) — to eat into or wear away, especially soil or rock

extinct (ex TINKT) — no longer existing

fertile (FUR til) — an area in which plants grow easily

humidity (hu MID ih tee) — wetness or moisture in the air

lumber (LUHM ber) — wood used in the building process

species (SPEE sheez) — a certain kind of plant or animal within a closely related group; for example, a *red-eyed* tree frog

INDEX

On the God of the Christians

Other Titles of interest from St. Augustine's Press